junk yard dogs

and William Shakespeare

As true a dog as ever
fought at head.

Titus Andronicus, V.i

junk yard dogs

and William Shakespeare

Photographs by Mark Lamonica

Woodford Press
San Francisco

This book is dedicated to my father, Louis Lamonica (1927-1997), to Joyce Caruso for loving me, to Sheldon Abend for guiding me and Puck, my dog, for coming up with the idea. And special thanks to Laurence Hyman for making it a reality.

Puck

For further reading: All Shakespeare's quotes used herein are identified by play, act, scene (ie: *Twelfth Night*, I.v).

Published by
WOODFORD PRESS
(a division of Woodford Publishing, Inc.)

660 Market Street, Suite 206
San Francisco, CA 94104

Book design by Laurence J. Hyman and Jim Santore.
Text edited by Wendy L. Gardner and David Lilienstein.

ISBN: 0-942627-44-4
Library of Congress Catalog Number: 97-60972
First Printing: September 1997
Printed and bound in the Uniited States of America
Distributed to the trade by National Book Network

INTRODUCTION

What is the connection between junkyard dogs and the great William Shakespeare? Well, admittedly, it is not a connection that leaps easily to mind. But, really, it makes perfect sense.

As a long-time student of The Bard, I can tell you that dogs of all kinds seem to have held a fascination and a charm for him. Indeed, dogs may even have been an obsession for him. The works of William Shakespeare are rife with mentions of dogs—as symbols, as comic relief, as metaphors.

The Bard knew his dogs.

He knew as modern anthropologists have documented time and again that man and canine have been symbiotic through the ages. He knew that the minute man domesticated the dog, the dog became his protector, helper, hunter and loyal companion, giving man breathing room to use his mind. Clearly, the relationship between man and dog was an endless source of inspiration for Shakespeare.

Of course, Shakespeare didn't know a junkyard as we know it, as some sprawling urban blight enclosed by a rotting fence and faithfully and formidably guarded by, yes, a "junkyard dog." But The Bard did know junkyards; the concept predates the machine age. He knew emotional and moral junkyards and, somehow, there always seemed to be a dog on the scene.

How do I fit into this?

I have been an artist since I was a child. I have owned many dogs. In the course of putting together this book, I have come to know thousands of dogs. As an artist I share my studio with my four dogs. I have a welding shop with chop saws and arc welders. The sound of grinding and the cracking of atoms are the music of my universe. As I work, my dogs stand as guardians at the gates, like the "hounds of Hecate," progenitor of Shakespeare's dogs. I am forever in their world, the metal grave-yards, the auto morgues, the junkyards, looking for material to sculpt and photograph.

Scholars galore take cracks at trying to unravel the magic of Shakespeare. The rest of us know what it is like to have been force-fed Shakespeare in high school. It was tough duty. I have traveled all over the United States photographing junkyard dogs. These are the dogs that Shakespeare refers to, the dogs of war that guard the castle gates.

"The totality of knowledge, all questions, all answers, reside in a dog," wrote Kafka. That is not a difficult notion for me to accept. It is the dogs—after 30 years of research—that teach me about myself, about life, about art and, the ultimate trick, about William Shakespeare.

Thaddeus Taylor, president of The Shakespeare Society of America, wrote to me: "Mark Lamonica, you have built the 'better mouse trap,' that even Hamlet paraphrases, by introducing Shakespearean characters into the animal kingdom. I congratulate you on something long overdue. I recommend your book highly. It is indeed a new way to teach and advance the works of Shakespeare."

I can live with that.

—MARK LAMONICA
New York City
Summer, 1997

I am the dog: no, the dog is himself, and I am the dog—Oh! the dog is me, and I am myself.

The Two Gentlemen of Verona, II.iii

Whose will stands but mine? There's none protector of the realm but I.

Henry IV, Part I, I.iii

9

You, O the dearest of creatures, would even renew me with your eyes.

Cymbeline, III.ii

Deep-drawing barks do
there disgorge
Their warlike fraughtage.

Troilus and Cressida, Prol.

The dog all this while sheds not a tear nor speaks a word.

The Two Gentlemen of Verona, II.iii

Talks as familiarly of roaring lions
As maids of thirteen do of puppy dogs.

King John, II.i

The venom clamors
of a jealous woman
Poison more deadly than a
mad dog's tooth.

Comedy of Errors, V.i

For I have neither wit, nor words, nor worth,
Action, nor utterance, nor the power of speech,
To stir men's blood; I only speak right on.

Julius Caesar, III.ii

Two curs shall tame each other.

Troilus and Cressida, I.iii

What is he at the gate, cousin?
-A gentleman.

Twelfth Night, I.v

Like a gate of steel
Fronting the Sun,
receives and renders back
His Figure and his heat.

Troilus and Cressida, III.iii

Hark, hark! Bow-wow.
The watch-dogs bark.

Tempest, I.ii

By your furtherance I am cloth'd in steel...

Pericles, Prince of Tyre, II.i

Had your watch been good, This sudden mischief never could have fall'n.

Henry VI, Part I, II.i

You may stroke him as gently
as a puppy greyhound.

Henry IV, Part II, II.iv

Hold you the watch to-night?
We do, my lord.

Hamlet, I.ii

24

Eye of newt and toe of frog,
Wool of bat and tongue of dog.

Macbeth, IV.i

'Out with the dog!' says one: 'What
cur is that? says another.

The Two Gentlemen of Verona, IV.iv

For all this flattering gloss,
He will be found a dangerous
protector.

Henry VI, Part II, I.i

I dare not fight; but I will wink
and hold out mine iron.

The Life of Henry V, II.i

He's a good dog, and a fair dog—can there be more said?

The Merry Wives of Windsor, I.i

WARNING

NO TRESPASSING

CPC 602

GUARD DOG ON DUTY

Hence! home, you idle creatures, get you home:
Is this a holiday?

Julius Caesar, I.i

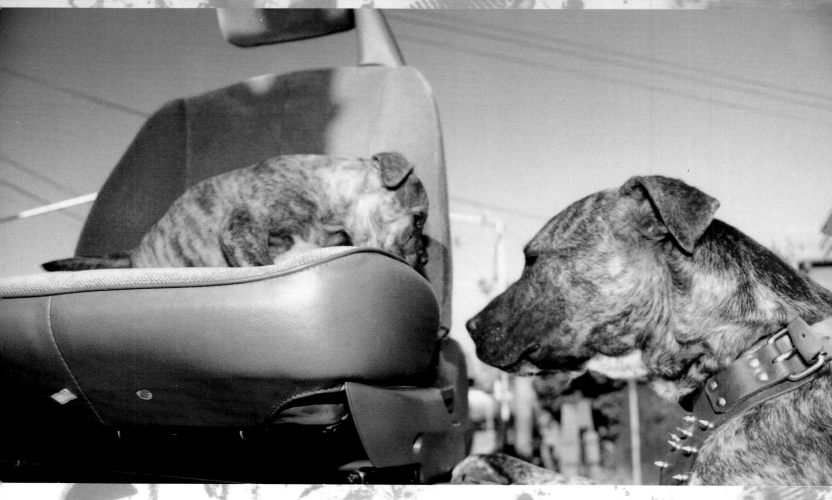

It is a wise father that knows his own child.

The Merchant of Venice, II.ii

'Tis a foul thing when a cur cannot keep himself in all companies.

The Two Gentlemen of Verona, IV.iv

Who do prepare to meet him at the gates,
There to give up their power.

Measure for Measure, IV.iii

Winding up days with toil and nights with sleep
Had the fore-hand and vantage of a king.

The Life of Henry V, IV.i

Thou call'dst me dog before thou hadst a cause,
But, since I am a dog, beware my fangs.

Merchant of Venice, III.iii

I do wish thou wert a dog,
That I might love thee something.

The Life of Timon of Athens, IV.iii

I have the wit to think my master is a kind of a knave.

The Two Gentlemen of Verona III.i

These eyes, like lamps whose wasting
oil is spent,
Wax dim.

Henry VI, Part I, II.v

Alack, there lies more peril in thine eye
Than twenty of their swords...

Romeo and Juliet, II.ii

Snarl, and bite, and play the dog.
Henry VI, V.vi

I am as ugly as a bear;
For beasts that meet me run away for fear.

A Midsummer Night's Dream, II.ii

43

One that takes upon him to be a dog indeed, to be, as it were, a dog at all things.

The Two Gentlemen of Verona, IV.iv

44

A king of shreds
and patches.

Hamlet, III.iv

How many goodly creatures are there here!
How beauteous mankind is!

Tempest, V.i

Fell into a sadness, then into a fast,
Thence to a watch.

Hamlet, II.ii

47

I offered her mine own, who is a dog as big as ten of yours.

The Two Gentlemen of Verona, IV.iv

In your protectorship you did devise
Strange tortures for offenders.

Henry IV, Part II, III.i

I am weary; yea, my memory is tired.
Have we no wine here?

Coriolanus, I.ix

My hounds are bred
out of the spartan kind;
So flew'd, so sanded;
their heads are hung
With ears that sweep
away the morning dew...

A Midsummer Night's Dream, IV.i

I heard you were saucy at my gates.

Twelfth Night, I.v

I have watch'd so long That I am dog-weary.

The Taming of the Shrew, IV.ii

Though this be madness yet there is method in't.

Hamlet, II.ii

Ay, every inch a king!

King Lear, IV.vi

Hell is empty,
And all the devils are here.

Tempest, I.ii

I had rather hear my dog bark at a crow than a man swear he loves me.

Much Ado About Nothing, I.i

Let Hercules himself do what he may,
The cat will mew, and dog will have his day.

Hamlet, V.i

Cowards die many times
before their deaths,
The valiant never taste of
death but once.

Julius Caesar, II.ii

O, I see that nose of yours, but not that dog I shall throw it to.

Othello, IV.i

A fond and desperate creature,
Whom sometime I have laugh'd with.

All's Well That Ends Well, V.iii

He hath eaten me out of house and home.

Henry IV, Part II, II.i

More straining on for
plucking back, not following
My leash unwillingly.

The Winter's Tale, IV.iv

65

With joy, pleasance, revel and applause,
transform ourselves into beasts!

Othello, II.iii

67

Open the gates unto the lord protector,
Or we'll burst them open.

Henry IV, Part I, I.iii

Pity the dearth that I have pined in,
By longing for that food so long a time.

The Two Gentlemen of Verona, II.vii

What valour were it, when a cur doth grin,
For one to thrust his hand between his teeth?

Henry IV, Part III, I.iv

Time shall unfold what plighted cunning hides.

King Lear, I.i

God and our innocence defend and guard us!

Richard III, III.v

That it shall hold companionship in peace
With honor, as in war.

Coriolanus, III.ii

Patience is sottish, and impatience does
Become a dog that's mad.

Antony and Cleopatra, IV.xv

Curse not thyself, fair creature.

Richard III, I.ii

Good night, lieutenant; I must to the watch.

Othello, II.iii

A peace above all earthly dignities, A still and quiet conscience.

Henry VIII, III.ii

Away, thou issue of a mangy dog!

The Life of Timon of Athens, IV.iii

Cry Havoc! and let slip the dogs of war.

Julius Caesar, III.i

Other men have gates and those gates open'd,
As mine, against their will.

The Winter's Tale, I.ii

Trust me, I take him for the better dog.

The Taming of the Shrew, Ind.i

Doubt thou the stars are fire, Doubt that the sun doth move,
Doubt truth to be a liar, But never doubt I love.

Hamlet, II.ii

Then I am no two-legged creature.

Henry IV, Part I, II.iv

I do follow here in the chase, not like a hound that hunts, but one that fills up the cry.

Othello, II.iii

We are beastly, subtle as the fox for prey,
Like warlike as the wolf.

Cymbeline, III.iii

To the platform, masters; Come, let's set the watch.

Othello, II.iii

They have tied me to a stake;
I cannot fly,
But bear-like I must fight the
course.

Macbeth, V.vii

Watch thou and wake
when others be asleep.

Henry VI, Part II, I.i

Uncover, dogs, and lap. What does his
lordship mean?

Timon of Athens, III.vi

The gods themselves,
Humbling their deities to love, have taken
The shapes of beasts upon them.

The Winter's Tale, II.iiii.

Apt enough to dislocate and tear
Thy flesh and bones.

King Lear, IV.ii

Ah, beastly creature! The blot and enemy to
our general name!

Titus Andronicus, II.iii

Woodford Press
a division of Woodford Publishing, Inc.
660 Market Street, Suite 206
San Francisco, California 94104
(415) 397-1853

Laurence J. Hyman, *Publisher and Creative Director*
C. David Burgin, *Editor and General Manager*
David Lilienstein, *V.P. Marketing and Development*
Jim Santore, *Art Director*
Wendy L. Gardner, *Assistant to the Editor*
Tony Khing, *Special Sales*
Debbie Fong, *Marketing Assistant*

Mark Lamonica is an internationally collected photographer, sculptor and welder. He shares his studio in Altadena, California with four dogs, who stand as guardians at the gates. On his travels across the country, he has been forever in the world of the junkyard, looking for material to sculpt and photograph. It was during these travels that he had the idea to meld his dog photographs with Shakespeare. Mr. Lamonica resides in both Brooklyn and Los Angeles.